Revised and Updated

People of New York

Mark Stewart

Heinemann Library
Chicago, Illinois

HEINEMANN-RAINTREE

TO ORDER:

☎ Phone Customer Service **888-454-2279**

💻 Visit **www.heinemannraintree.com** to browse our catalog and order online.

Editorial: Megan Cotugno
Design: Kimberly R. Miracle, Betsy Wernert, Ryan Frieson
Photo Research: Tracy Cummins
Production: Alison Parsons

Originated by Chroma Graphics Pte Ltd.
Printed and bound in China by Leo Paper Group
The paper used to print this book comes from
sustainable resources.

ISBN-13: 978-1-4329-1133-1 (hc)
ISBN-10: 1-4329-1133-3 (hc)
ISBN-13: 978-1-4329-1140-9 (pb)
ISBN-10: 1-4329-1140-6 (pb)

13 12 11 10 09 08
10 9 8 7 6 5 4 3 2 1

**The Library of Congress has cataloged the first edition
as follows:**
Stewart, Mark, 1960-
  People of New York : New York state studies /
Mark Stewart.
      p. cm.
Summary: Examines the diversity of peoples who inhabit
New York State, including ethnic groups and immigrants,
and profiles such famous New Yorkers as Susan B.
Anthony, George Gershwin, and Jackie Robinson.
  Includes bibliographical references and index.
ISBN 978-1-4329-1133-1 (hc) --
ISBN 978-1-4329-1140-9 (pb) 1. Ethnology--New York
(State)--Juvenile literature. 2. New York (State)--Juvenile
literature. [1. New York (State)--Population. 2. Ethnology--
New York (State). 3. Minorities--New York (State). 4.
Immigrants--New York (State). 5. New York (State)--
Biography.] I. Title.
  F130.A1S74 2003
  974.7'009'9--dc21
                                2002154310

Acknowledgments
The author and publishers are grateful to the following for
permission to reproduce copyright material:
**pp. 4, 20, 21, 26, 27, 30, 32, 37T, 39, 40, 41, 42,
44** ©Bettmann/Corbis; **p. 5** ©Don Emmert/AFP/Getty
Images; **pp. 7, 9, 45** ©Maps.com/Heinemann Library; **pp.
8, 10, 13T, 15** ©The Granger Collection, New York; **pp.
11, 19, 34, 35, 43** ©Corbis; **pp. 13B, 37B** ©Reuters
NewMedia Inc./Corbis; **p. 14** ©Frances Roberts / Alamy;
p. 16 ©Marty Lederhandler/AP Wide World Photos; **p.
17** ©Gail Mooney/Corbis; **p. 22** ©Chip East/Reuters/
Corbis; **p. 23T** ©Ted S. Warren/AP Wide World Photos;
p. 23B ©Kathy Willens/AP Wide World Photos; **p. 24T**
©Jean Chung/AP Wide World Photos; **p. 24B** ©Shannon
Stapleton/Reuters/Corbis; **p. 25** ©AP Wide World Photos;
p. 28 ©Museum of the City of New York/Corbis; **p. 29**
Mark Von Holden/Getty Images; **p. 31** ©Underwood &
Underwood/Corbis; **p. 33T** ©Matthew Cavanaugh/epa/
Corbis; **p. 33B** ©Archivo Iconografico, S.A./Corbis; **p. 36**
©George Widman/AP Wide World Photos; **p. 38** ©J. Scott
Applewhite/AP Wide World Photos

Cover Image reproduced with permission of ©Getty
Images/Tatsuya Morita.

The publishers would like to thank Nancy Harris for her
assistance in the preparation of this book.

Every effort has been made to contact copyright holders
of any material reproduced in this book. Any omissions
will be rectified in subsequent printings if notice is given
to the publisher.

Disclaimer
All the Internet addresses (URLs) given in this book were
valid at the time of going to press. However, due to the
dynamic nature of the Internet, some addresses may
have changed, or sites may have changed or ceased to
exist since publication. While the author and publisher
regret any inconvenience this may cause readers, no
responsibility for any such changes can be accepted by
either the author or the publisher.

Contents

Some words are shown in bold, **like this**. You can find out what they mean by looking in the glossary.

The People of New York

New York used to be called the nation's great "melting pot." In centuries past, people from every country, race, and religion came to New York and tried their best to fit in with everyone else. Sometimes, that meant changing their name, hiding their accent, getting used to strange food, or listening to unfamiliar music. To be a New Yorker meant to "melt" their traits with the **culture** to become the same as everyone else.

Today, New York is more like a magnet. It attracts people from all over the world, yet these people no longer want to erase their past. Now New York is a celebration of **diversity**. It draws its energy and its strength from the differences of its many people. In New York City alone, more than 200 different languages are spoken.

Street markets were popular in the 1900s in New York City's Lower East Side as **immigrants** sold and bought goods.

New York's Census Data

In 2000 the U.S. **Census** reported that 18,976,457 people live in the state of New York. New York is the third-largest state in the nation in population, behind California and Texas. New York also has the largest city in population in the nation—New York City.

The U.S. Census also counts the number of people of each race within a state. Out of every 100 people in the state of New York, approximately 70 are Caucasian, 16 are African American, 6 are Asian, 15 are Latino, and 10 are of a different race or a combination of several races.

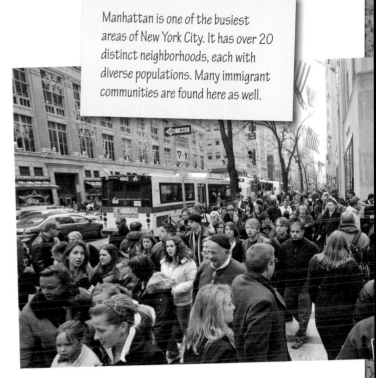

Manhattan is one of the busiest areas of New York City. It has over 20 distinct neighborhoods, each with diverse populations. Many immigrant communities are found here as well.

New York's Demographics: 1990 vs. 2000

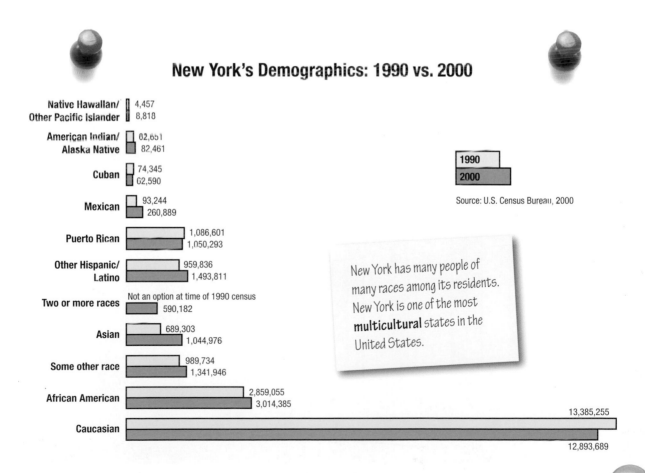

	1990	2000
Native Hawaiian/Other Pacific Islander	4,457	8,818
American Indian/Alaska Native	62,651	82,461
Cuban	74,345	62,590
Mexican	93,244	260,889
Puerto Rican	1,086,601	1,050,293
Other Hispanic/Latino	959,836	1,493,811
Two or more races	Not an option at time of 1990 census	590,182
Asian	689,303	1,044,976
Some other race	989,734	1,341,946
African American	2,859,055	3,014,385
Caucasian	13,385,255	12,893,689

Source: U.S. Census Bureau, 2000

New York has many people of many races among its residents. New York is one of the most **multicultural** states in the United States.

5

People can be of different **ethnicities** as well. The people who have immigrated to New York bring their **cultural heritage** to the state. Over 125,000 new immigrants come to New York every year. Also, nearly one of every three of New York's children are either foreign-born or the child of an immigrant.

Where Do New Yorkers Live?

New York is a large place—over 54,000 square miles (140,000 square kilometers)—but nearly half the state's population is crowded into the New York City **metropolitan** area. According to the 2000 U.S. Census, over 8 million people live in New York City. A 2005 estimate put the city's population at over 8.1 million. Buffalo is the next largest city in New York in population, and it only has 292,648 people.

Top Ten New York Cities by Population: 1990 vs. 2000

New York's ten largest cities have a wide range of population sizes. New York City has over 8 million people, while Utica has only 60,000!

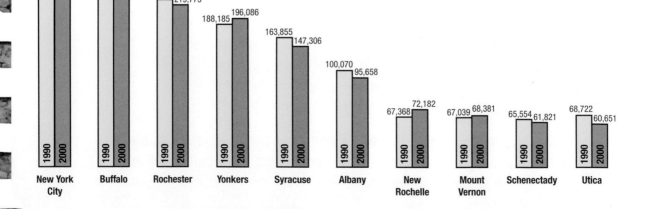

City	1990	2000
New York City	7,322,564	8,008,278
Buffalo	327,931	292,648
Rochester	230,872	219,773
Yonkers	188,185	196,086
Syracuse	163,855	147,306
Albany	100,070	95,658
New Rochelle	67,368	72,182
Mount Vernon	67,039	68,381
Schenectady	65,554	61,821
Utica	68,722	60,651

New York
Population Change
by County: 1990 vs. 2000

Lake Ontario

Lake Erie

0   50 miles
0   50 km

Population Change

- Population gain
- Population loss

New York state experienced a lot of population movement in the ten years between 1990 and 2000. About half of the counties lost residents while the other half gained residents.

New York has a total of 62 counties. The counties with the biggest populations are found where there are many **industries** to employ workers. Counties in the New York City area include Rockland, Orange, Westchester, Bronx, Dutchess, Kings, Putnam, Queens, and Richmond. All experienced a large growth in population between 1990 and 2000.

Both the immigrants and the people who were born and raised in the state contribute to making the state a melting pot of all cultures. It is this blend of people with ties to places all over the world that makes New York a **diverse** state.

Origins of New York's People

Around 3500 BCE, members of a Native American mound-building **culture** lived in the area. Their culture stretched from the Mississippi River to the Atlantic Ocean. They hunted, fished, and gathered plants for food. Toward the end of their stay in New York, they began growing corn and other crops. The mound builders were long gone when the first European explorers arrived. By that time, the Iroquois and Algonquin tribes had settled in the region. They knew nothing of the native peoples who had lived there before them.

A baby sleeps on a papoose board while the Iroquois women grind corn and berries.

Algonquin longhouses were built on Manhattan Island before the Dutch settled the area.

New York Reservations

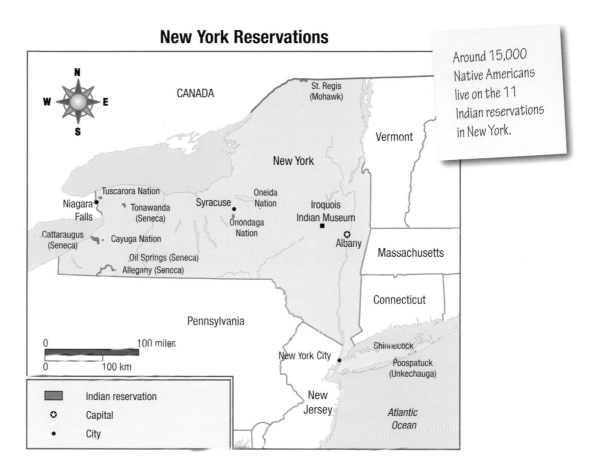

Around 15,000 Native Americans live on the 11 Indian reservations in New York.

The Algonquins and Iroquois occupied the vast territory stretching from the Atlantic Ocean to the Great Lakes for many centuries before the arrival of the Europeans. The Iroquois lands included most of northern and western New York, while the Algonquins lived near the ocean and along the Hudson River.

In the late 1500s, five tribes—the Mohawks, Oneidas, Onondagas, Cayugas, and Senecas—banded together to form the Iroquois League. A sixth tribe, the Tuscaroras, joined later, after they were driven from their land in North Carolina. This was the situation when the Dutch established their first colony, New Netherland, in 1624. From that time forward, the Native Americans lost more and more of their land to European settlers.

Today, more than 80,000 Native Americans live in New York. New York City has the largest Native American population of any major **metropolitan** area in the United States.

Dutch

The makeup of New York has been different from other parts of the United States ever since it was established as a colony. Unlike other British colonies, the Dutch settlement of New Amsterdam on Manhattan Island was made up of people from many different places. Some of them included France, Belgium, England, Germany, and Scandinavia. In the 1640s, when the population of New Amsterdam was around 1,000, more than 15 languages could be heard in the streets and stores. New Amsterdam's early history predicted what New York's future would hold.

People of different nationalities who were searching for new opportunities found hope in New Netherland.

The first settlement in Rochester, New York, was established in 1812. Today, Rochester is home to over 200,000 people.

Although the British took over the colony of New Netherland in 1664, many Dutch continued to live there. By 1700, when the colony's population had grown to 15,000, at least half of all New Yorkers were Dutch. Many Dutch people lived in the North. Here, powerful landowners called *patroons* ran huge farms and **dominated** politics around Albany and Kingston.

British

In New York City, British influence grew quickly. By 1750, the city's population had reached 25,000, and most of those people were of British origin. However, since New York City was the busiest seaport in the colonies, it was also the most international city. Although no official **statistics** were kept until the 1850s, historians think that many kinds of people—from Asia, Europe, South America, and Africa—were living in the city during the years after the American Revolution, which ended in 1783.

Irish

A wave of **immigration** began in the 1780s and lasted through the 1820s. Many people came from **rural** areas of Ireland and Scotland. The majority of these Scotch-Irish settlers were too poor to buy land near cities, so many of them moved west within New York, where land was still free. They formed dozens of villages throughout the state.

Irish immigrants fled the Potato **Famine** and terrible poverty in Ireland and sailed to America to start new lives.

The First Wave

What was going on in Europe in the early 1800s that made people want to leave their homelands and come to the U.S.? It was not one thing, but a combination of powerful forces. For centuries, the life of a European villager had changed little. In the early 1800s, however, life began to change quickly.

The population in Europe doubled between 1700 and 1800. This meant that there was less land, less food, and less opportunity for the people who lived there. In the early 1800s, many poor farmers were forced to stop farming and start working in factories, and many were unable to adjust to this new way of life.

Letters from friends and family in the U.S. provided hope to these people. They spoke of a land that stretched to the horizon—much of it free for those willing to farm it. After the American Revolution (1775–1783), the United States was a place where rich and poor had to follow the same laws. Leaders were elected (chosen) by the people and people were free to worship any religion they liked. Many people saw the United States as a country that offered all the things their own country did not.

For a period of time after 1790, ship battles made the Atlantic Ocean unsafe for travel. During this time, Europe was undergoing a population explosion. Food, money, and housing were hard to come by. When travel again became safe, thousands of people started coming to the United States. The offers of freedom and land here were very tempting for many Irish people. Hardworking Irishmen had been working in British and Scottish factories for decades, but because of a downturn in business, they were sent back to Ireland. When famines hit Ireland, people grew desperate for food. With offers of wages of up to $2 a day in the United States, thousands braved the ocean voyage from the mid-1840s to the early 1850s. New York's Irish newcomers found work digging **canals** and building railroads. They also worked in the state's factories and along city waterfronts.

Irish immigration continued right into the 1900s. This group spread out across the growing nation, and is represented in every part of the United States today. In New York state, several towns retain the same **ethnic** feel they had in the 1800s. This is true particularly in the state capital of Albany, where the Irish settled in the years after the Erie Canal was completed.

In the Catskills, the village of East Durham has been a favorite summer retreat of Irish-Americans for many years. Each March, Irish culture is celebrated in the St. Patrick's Day parade, a New York City tradition since 1752. The state's other major St. Patrick's Day parade takes place in Buffalo.

People of all **cultures** come out to celebrate St. Patrick's Day in New York City.

Germans

In Germany, political **turmoil** caused a great wave of immigration to the United States. Some immigrants were **peasants** who lost their land or craftspeople who could not compete with new factories. German immigrants were better off than the Irish, but not by much. Many Germans had useful craft skills, which the Irish did not have. Most Germans were educated. Some came with enough money to start businesses.

Polish

Buffalo also holds one of the nation's largest Pulaski Day parades, which celebrates America's Polish **heritage**. The Poles were among the second wave of immigrants to come to New York. This wave began in the 1880s and lasted until the 1920s.

New York City also hosts a large Pulaski Day parade each year. These people marching in the parade are wearing traditional Polish clothing.

Polish people came to the United States to escape being drafted into the army, and because they were losing their land in Poland. Many Polish immigrants intended to be in the U.S. for only a short while, just to make some money before returning home. They took low-paying, unskilled jobs in factories because they did not usually have the training to get higher-paying jobs. However, when the farming problems did not improve in Poland, many immigrants decided to stay in the U.S.

The Second Wave

The second great wave of immigration, which lasted from the 1880s to the 1920s, was made possible by two U.S. inventions: the steamship and advertising. In the days of the sailing ship, it could take two months to reach the U.S. from some European **ports**. Thanks to steam-powered boats, the same voyage took less than two weeks. Also, because there were so many steamship companies competing for customers, the price of a **transatlantic** trip was less than $50. This included a railroad ticket from New York to a final destination.

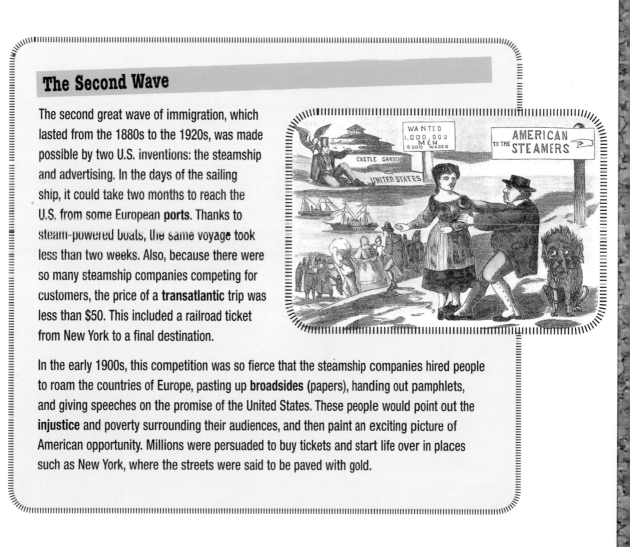

In the early 1900s, this competition was so fierce that the steamship companies hired people to roam the countries of Europe, pasting up **broadsides** (papers), handing out pamphlets, and giving speeches on the promise of the United States. These people would point out the **injustice** and poverty surrounding their audiences, and then paint an exciting picture of American opportunity. Millions were persuaded to buy tickets and start life over in places such as New York, where the streets were said to be paved with gold.

New York declared Columbus Day a holiday in 1909. Over 100,000 people, including many Italians, march each year in the parade down Fifth Avenue in New York City.

Italians

The majority of the newcomers during this period were from southern and eastern Europe. Of these newcomers, most were from Italy. During the early 1800s, only a few thousand Italian immigrants entered the United States. However, Italy's population exploded during the 1800s. Poor soil and old-fashioned farming techniques could not grow enough food to feed everyone in Italy. Toward the end of the 1800s, large numbers of Italians landed in New York every day. By the early 1900s, nearly a million people in New York City were Italian-Americans. This was more than the entire population of Rome, Italy, at that time!

Most of these Italian immigrants were young men who were willing to work hard and live cheaply, and many wanted to return to Italy one day with their savings. They filled jobs that demanded twelve or more hours of work each day, ranging from construction jobs to working as pushcart vendors. As they moved north and west, they settled into towns across New York state. Today, the cities of Utica, Rome, and Buffalo still have an Italian atmosphere. Across New York, Italian restaurants, festivals, and the popular Columbus Day parade that is held in many cities keep the culture alive.

Ellis Island

Although the immigrants in the second wave came into the country through several ports, the vast majority arrived at Ellis Island in New York Harbor. Completed in 1892, Ellis Island had two purposes. The first was to keep some people out of the United States. Anyone who showed signs of disease or mental illness—or who was suspected of being a criminal—was shipped back home. The second purpose of Ellis Island was to document how many people were entering the United States, who they were, and where they were coming from.

Because 10,000 or more immigrants were processed each day, the first examination given to newly arrived travelers lasted only a few seconds. Those who were obviously sick were sent to one of the many hospital buildings on the island. Then came the interview, during which people were asked questions about their home, their **prospects** for work, and their final destination. This was a scary experience—many believed that a wrong answer could lead to **deportation**—but no one knew exactly which answers the inspectors at Ellis Island wanted to hear.

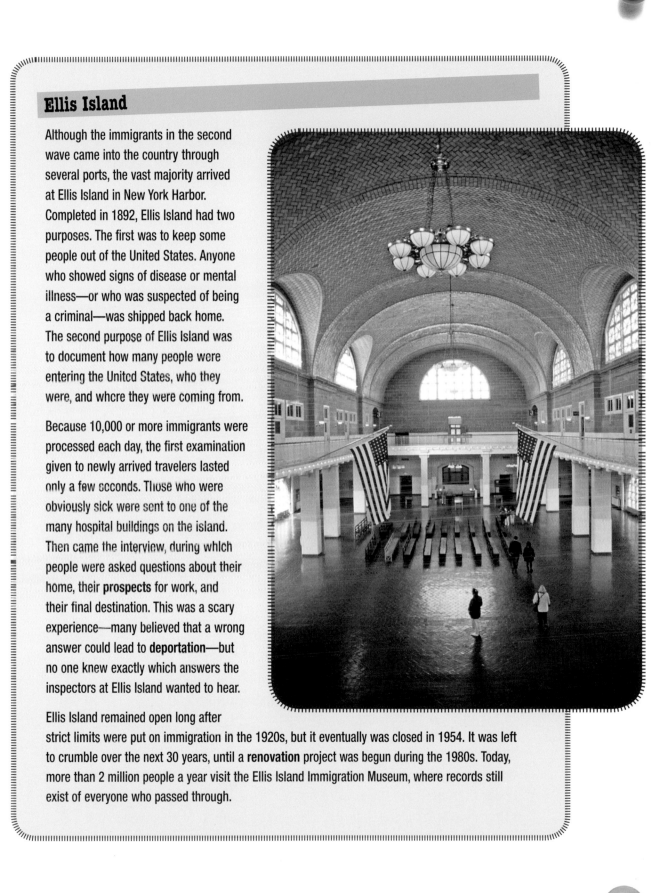

Ellis Island remained open long after strict limits were put on immigration in the 1920s, but it eventually was closed in 1954. It was left to crumble over the next 30 years, until a **renovation** project was begun during the 1980s. Today, more than 2 million people a year visit the Ellis Island Immigration Museum, where records still exist of everyone who passed through.

Jews

During the period from 1880 to 1920, approximately 3.5 million Jewish immigrants passed through New York Harbor. The European Jews settled in New York for a few reasons. New York was seen as a land of opportunity, and it had a **diverse** immigrant community. Each culture was facing the same problems as the Jews, such as poverty and adjusting to a new way of life.

The Jewish immigrants who arrived were mostly manual workers in their old countries. Most of the immigrants worked in unfavorable conditions in the clothing **industry** when they came to America. Others took to the streets, selling goods in pushcarts and stores.

African Americans

African Americans make up the second largest ethnic group in New York, but few came through Ellis Island. New York's first black residents arrived as the slaves of Dutch merchants. They were among the first settlers in New Amsterdam. Records show that there were eleven in all when the Dutch first arrived, but more soon followed. A generation later, the Dutch declared their slaves free and gave them land to live on at the northern end of the island of Manhattan.

Unfortunately, this freedom did not last long. When the British took over in the 1660s, Manhattan became the country's second-largest slave market. Soon there were more slaves in New York than in any other northern colony. Many of the slaves were in or near New York City. Roughly one in five city residents was a slave in the years prior to the American Revolution (1775–1783).

After the British left the city in the 1780s, freedom did not come for New York's African Americans as quickly as expected. A gradual **emancipation** act was passed by the state **legislature** in 1799, but it was not until 1827 that slavery was finally **abolished** in the state. In the years that followed, most white New Yorkers were not eager to fight against the slavery that still existed in the South. New York did a lot of business with the cotton growers in that region. They did not want to see the slaves freed because without slave labor, their business costs would go up.

Despite the state's uncertain feelings toward slavery, New York became part of the **Underground Railroad** for escaping slaves. Aided by free blacks in New York City and white **abolitionists** throughout the state, runaway slaves could make their way into Canada across the Niagara River. It was a long and dangerous journey, but more than 20,000 made it. The port cities of Rochester and Oswego were important stops on the Underground Railroad.

Harriet Tubman, of Auburn, was one of the conductors of the Underground Railroad. She helped over 300 slaves reach freedom in Canada.

Southern politicians were furious with New York for aiding escaped slaves and threatened to slow the flow of goods to the North. New York lawmakers agreed to support the Fugitive Slave Act which made it a **federal** crime to help escapees. However, this did little to slow the abolitionist movement. In 1851 antislavery **vigilantes** attacked federal marshals who had arrested escaped slave Jerry McHenry in Syracuse. This event stayed in the mind of the public, and it became one of many events that helped to start the Civil War in 1861.

During and after the Civil War (1861–1865), New York's African-American population grew as many former slaves looked for a better life in the North. Some found success in business, but most found it difficult to get jobs that paid well. Slowly, a solid working class started to develop, especially in Manhattan. Still, it was not until the early years of the 1900s that the state's African-American population began to **thrive**.

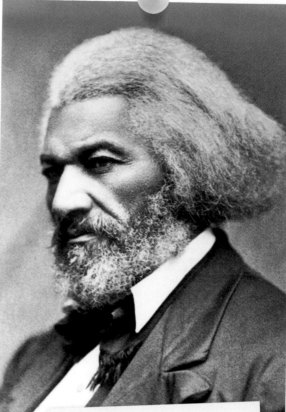

Frederick Douglass was a leading abolitionist. He settled in Rochester and published a newspaper called *The North Star*. This newspaper informed people about the antislavery movement throughout the country.

In the 1880s and 1890s, New York City's Harlem neighborhood had attracted many wealthy white families. Harlem is located at the northern end of Central Park, which at that time was a quiet, out-of-the-way place. In 1901 the IRT **subway** line was extended up Lenox Avenue into the heart of this area. Real estate investors believed New Yorkers would flock to Harlem, and they built thousands of **brownstones**. When house sales were slower than they expected, they feared they would lose the money they had spent to build the houses.

The creative and intellectual activity of the African-American community in Harlem became known as the Harlem Renaissance.

An African-American realtor approached the developers and offered to fill the townhouses with all the renters they needed. Because of their skin color, it was impossible for black families to find decent housing elsewhere in the city. The developers jumped at this offer. Within 20 years, Harlem, with its beautiful architecture and tree-lined, busy streets, became the center of African-American culture in New York.

There were many places where mixed-race audiences enjoyed the incredible talent that flowed from this community. One of the most popular among them was the Apollo Theater. Between the 1930s and 1960s, everyone from Billie Holiday to the Jackson Five performed music there. Wednesday night was **Amateur** Night, an evening tradition for many years. After years of neglect, the Apollo was restored to its original beauty.

Amateur Night at the Apollo Theater was a time to have the stage and show off special talents. Here, young musicians perform for the audience.

New York's African-American population made great progress in the job world between the 1920s and 1950s. This was partly because work was easier to find. In the 1920s, the U.S. government placed strict limitations on immigration. This meant that there were fewer newcomers willing to work hard for low wages. Employers that had once **discriminated** against African Americans now began to hire them. Although the African-American community was hit just as hard by the **Great Depression** as others were, these new jobs brought some economic and political power to people who before had neither.

Although the new immigration laws helped one group of New Yorkers, it discriminated against others. Very few Asians and Latinos were allowed into the country during that time period. The face of New York was again **transformed** by these new laws. Finally, in 1965, the restrictions were eased. This began a third wave of immigration that continues to this day.

New York City is the top destination for new immigrants arriving in the United States, with 1.3 million arriving between 1990 and 2000.

Immigrant neighborhoods maintain some of the traditions of their home countries. In Chinatown, people buy groceries at local markets. In Little Italy, people gather to play bocce ball.

Immigrants Today

New York City is world-famous for its different ethnic neighborhoods. Somewhere in the city there is a place where immigrants know they can find a familiar meal or newspaper, or where family and friends have already found a home.

Because immigrants typically work long hours for low pay, it can take many years before they can afford to move away from the city. During this time, they improve their English and start to blend old traditions and new. They become part of New York's huge human **tapestry**. This is when tightly knit ethnic neighborhoods form. Many people like to live in a place where they share a common experience with their neighbors.

As people in an ethnic group gain more power and influence, through owning businesses and getting involved in politics, they often leave their old neighborhood. They maintain close ties through traditional gatherings and with phone calls or emails. Meanwhile, a newer immigrant group moves into the old neighborhood, and the process begins again.

Nearly 200 ethnic newspapers and magazines are printed in New York City. Immigrants can easily find a publication in their language.

Today, New York's older immigrant groups, including the Irish, Germans, Italians, and eastern Europeans, have been almost completely absorbed. Their last names are still easy to recognize, but gone are the accents and old-country customs that once made them stand out. They live and work throughout the state.

Saying the Pledge of Allegiance is one way to unite all people living in the United States, whether they were born here or came from another country.

Newer immigrant groups are as anxious as those who came before them to become tried-and-true New Yorkers, but they want to do so on their own terms. Proud of their homelands and heritage, they believe in a **multicultural** United States. Like New York's earliest pioneers, they want to make a country that is proud to have them and of which they themselves can be proud.

Famous New Yorkers

New York has been home to thousands of famous Americans. Some were born in the Empire State, while others gained fame and fortune here. While it is impossible to list all famous New Yorkers, some of the most well known—past and present—are profiled in the following pages.

Bella Abzug

Abzug, Bella (1920–1998), social **activist**. A popular and outspoken **crusader** for women and the poor, Abzug was instantly recognizable in her trademark floppy hat. "Battling Bella" won a seat in Congress in 1971. She fought for human decency, fairness, and peace.

Anthony, Susan B. (1820–1906), social activist. Anthony came to Rochester, New York, as a teacher in 1845 and launched her career as a **reformer** soon after. Known for her tireless campaign to win the right to vote for women, she and Elizabeth Cady Stanton began the **Women's Rights Movement**.

Arthur, Chester Alan (1829–1886), politician. Arthur joined the Republican Party after moving to New York. He was nominated to run as James Garfield's vice president in 1880. Arthur became U.S. president when Garfield was **assassinated** in the summer of 1881. Arthur was an effective leader, but poor health prevented him from running for re-election in 1884.

James Baldwin

Baldwin, James (1924–1987), writer and social **activist**. Baldwin was a powerful voice in the **Civil Rights movement** of the 1960s. However, when three of his friends—Martin Luther King Jr., Malcolm X, and Medgar Evers—were murdered, he lost hope in the cause. He moved to France, and continued to write.

Ball, Lucille (1911–1989), actor. Ball, born near Jamestown, had a successful movie career before teaming up with her husband, Desi Arnaz, in 1951 to create the hit television comedy *I Love Lucy*. After the success of that show, Ball went on to perform in movies, Broadway productions, and other television shows she produced.

Beecher, Henry Ward (1813–1887), religious leader. After coming to the Plymouth Church of the Pilgrims in Brooklyn Heights in 1847, Beecher drew crowds with his antislavery sermons. By the start of the Civil War in 1861, he was one of America's best-known public figures.

Bellamy, Francis (1855–1931), editor, clergyman. Bellamy was born and raised in New York before moving to Boston as an adult. He wrote the Pledge of Allegiance, which was published on September 8, 1892. There was some question over who was the true author of the pledge, but in 1939, the U.S. Flag Association gave Bellamy the credit.

Bernstein, Leonard (1918–1990), music **composer** and **conductor**. Bernstein used television to bring classical music to a young audience in the 1950s and 1960s. He also wrote two New York musical theater classics: *On the Town* and *West Side Story*.

Brady, Matthew (1823–1896), photographer. Brady operated a successful photography studio in New York City for many years. At the outbreak of the Civil War (1861–1865), he closed his shop and traveled with the Union Army to **chronicle** the war. Although his photos made him famous, he died in poverty.

Burr, Aaron (1756–1836), politician. Burr was nearly elected New York's governor in 1804, and almost won the U.S. presidency four years before that. Alexander Hamilton, a political rival, contributed to Burr's defeat in his race for New York governor in 1804, so Burr killed Hamilton in a **duel**. Burr was involved in the planning of an illegal attack upon Spanish territory, and was charged with **treason**. He was found not guilty. He fled to Europe, returning to the United States in 1812.

Aaron Burr

Cardozo, Benjamin (1870–1938), judge. Known for his social **conscience** and understanding of the law, Cardozo was one of the most admired judges in the country. He was appointed to the U.S. Supreme Court by President Herbert Hoover in 1932, and served until his death in 1938.

Carrier, Willis (1876–1950), engineer, inventor. A graduate of Cornell University, in Ithaca, Carrier used his engineering degree to design a **humidity** control device. He soon became an expert in the science of "air conditioning" and formed the Carrier Corporation, which still makes air-conditioners today.

Cleveland, Grover (1837–1908), politician. Cleveland entered politics after moving to Buffalo, where he became known for his honesty and his support of the working class. He was elected U.S. president in 1884, but enemies kept him from winning re-election in 1888. Cleveland was re-elected as president in 1892.

Clinton, DeWitt (1769–1828), politician. The nephew of George Clinton, New York's first governor, DeWitt Clinton first made his mark when he organized the public school system as New York City mayor. During two terms as governor, and an unsuccessful run at the U.S. presidency, he pushed through the Erie **Canal** project that **transformed** life in New York.

Cole, Thomas (1801–1848), artist. Cole sailed to Philadelphia as a teenager, and in his thirties became famous for painting breathtaking landscapes. A founder of the **Hudson River school**, a style of landscape painting, he remains one of the most famous painters in the U.S.

DeWitt Clinton

Cooper, James Fenimore (1789–1851), author. Cooper's novels opened a window into the day-to-day lives of New Yorkers in the 1700s and early 1800s. His most famous novel, *Last of the Mohicans*, described a relationship between a **frontiersman**, Hawkeye, and a Native American, Chingachgook. His characters and style were copied by many other authors after him.

Cooper, Peter (1791–1883), businessperson, inventor. Cooper's companies built America's first steam engine, laid the first **transatlantic** telegraph cable, and invented the first washing machine. In 1858 he established New York City's Cooper Union, which offered free classes in the arts and technical sciences.

Copland, Aaron (1900–1990), composer. Influenced by popular music as well as the great classical works, Copland is considered by many to be the most original and important American composer of the 1900s.

Cuomo, Mario (b. 1932), social activist, politician. A tough but thoughtful community activist in the 1960s, Cuomo was New York's **lieutenant governor** for four years in the 1970s. He was then elected governor and served from 1983 to 1995. During his time in office, he became a well-spoken leader in the Democratic Party, but twice decided not to run for U.S. president.

Mario Cuomo

Davis, Sammy Jr. (1925–1990), entertainer. Born in Harlem, Davis made his stage debut at the age of three. At the age of seven, Davis appeared in his first film. As an adult, he became a popular performer, actor, singer, dancer, and impressionist.

New York Yankees players Vic Raschi (left), Joe DiMaggio (center), and Yogi Berra (right).

DiMaggio, Joe (1914–1999), athlete. The star of the Yankees from 1936 to 1951, DiMaggio led the baseball team to ten world championships. He is one New York's best loved sports heroes.

Douglass, Frederick (1818–1895), human rights activist, **orator**, and author. Born into slavery, Douglass escaped to New York when he was 20 and then moved to Massachusetts. After nearly a decade as an antislavery crusader, he returned to New York and published a newspaper called *The North Star*. Douglass convinced President Abraham Lincoln to use African-American soldiers in the Civil War (1861–1865) and fought for the rights of freed slaves in the years following that conflict.

Frederick Douglass

Eastman, George (1854–1932), inventor, manufacturer, and **philanthropist**. As Rochester's most famous citizen, Eastman put the magic of photography in the hands of the everyday person. He introduced the Kodak camera in 1888, and the Brownie camera in 1900, at prices so afforable almost everyone could buy one.

Ellington, Duke (1899–1974), musician. After moving to Harlem in the 1920s, Ellington composed pieces that blended the very different talents of his band members. He is still a legend in the world of jazz music.

Ferraro, Geraldine (b. 1935), lawyer, politician. The daughter of Italian **immigrants**, Ferraro was elected to Congress in 1978 after serving as assistant district attorney for the **borough** of Queens. She became the first woman to run for vice president of the United States for a major political party. Democrat Walter Mondale chose her as his running mate in the 1984 presidential election, which they lost.

Fillmore, Millard (1800–1874), lawyer, politician. A self-taught lawyer who served in the U.S. House of Representatives in the 1830s and 1840s, Fillmore became vice president of the United States when he ran for election with Zachary Taylor in 1848. Fillmore became president in 1850 when Taylor died in office. During his two years in the White House, he helped open relations with Japan and supported a law that guaranteed the return of escaped slaves to their owners. Fillmore lost the nomination of his party in 1852 because of his support of slavery, and he retired from politics soon after.

Garvey, Marcus (1887–1940), political activist. Garvey was the founder of the first black nationalist movement in the United States. He felt that African Americans would gain respect if they became **economically** strong, and he supported the idea of a separate country run by and for blacks in Africa.

Marcus Garvey

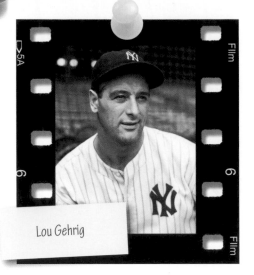

Lou Gehrig

Gehrig, Lou (1903–1941), athlete. Gehrig was one of baseball's greatest hitters. His streak of 2,130 games played for the New York Yankees ended when he contracted amyotrophic lateral sclerosis (ALS), which became known as Lou Gehrig's Disease. This disease makes it difficult to control one's muscles, which are eventually **paralyzed**.

Gellar, Sarah Michelle (b. 1977), actor. Gellar was discovered in a restaurant by a talent agent at the age of four. Since then, she has appeared in numerous television and movie roles, including playing Buffy in *Buffy the Vampire Slayer*.

Gershwin, George (1898–1937), music composer. George and his brother Ira borrowed from jazz and other music trends to transform popular and classical music in the 1920s and 1930s. George wrote the concert piece *Rhapsody in Blue* when he was only 25 years old.

Gibson, Althea (1927–2003), athlete. Raised in Harlem during the 1930s and 1940s, Gibson was already a paddle tennis champion before she picked up her first tennis racket. In 1957, she won the U.S. Nationals to become America's top-ranked player and Associated Press Athlete of the Year.

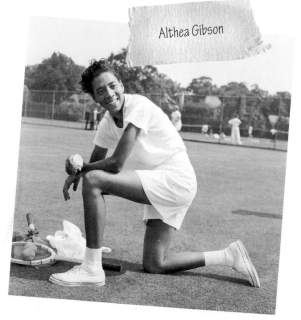

Althea Gibson

Ginsburg, Ruth Bader (b. 1933), attorney and judge. Though she possessed great talent and understanding of the law, Ginsburg was held back in the 1960s because she was a woman. She became the legal mind behind the women's rights movement, helping to change many **discriminatory** laws. In 1993, President Bill Clinton appointed Ginsburg to the U.S. Supreme Court.

Giuliani, Rudolph (b. 1944), politician. After becoming New York City's first Republican mayor in a generation, Giuliani cracked down on the city's crime. It dropped by 57 percent. He introduced a "Workfare" program that saved the city almost one billion dollars. After the terrorist attacks on September 11, 2001, Giuliani led New York City in its recovery efforts and was named *TIME* magazine's Person of the Year. He ran for U.S. president in the 2008 campaign.

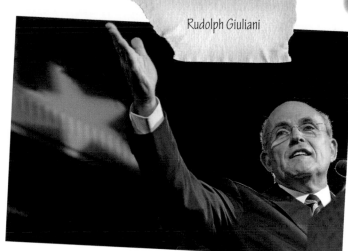

Rudolph Giuliani

Gould, Jay (1836–1892), railroad developer. Gould made a fortune **manipulating** railroad stocks and was labeled a **robber baron** in the 1860s. In 1869 he tried unsuccessfully to **corner** the nation's gold market and caused the stock market to crash.

Greeley, Horace (1811–1872), newspaper editor. Greeley began his publishing career as a typesetter. At the age of 30, he founded the *New York Tribune*, a successful newspaper that published antislavery articles.

Alexander Hamilton

Hamilton, Alexander (1757–1804), politician. A hero of the American Revolution and the first secretary of the treasury of the United States, Hamilton believed that his new country needed a strong government. In 1800 he prevented Aaron Burr from becoming president, and four years later blocked Burr's attempt to become New York's governor. Burr killed Hamilton in a duel in July of 1804.

Harriman, Averill (1891–1986), **diplomat** and politician. The son of a railroad **tycoon**, Harriman devoted his life to government and public service. He played important roles during the **Great Depression**, World War II (1939–1945), and the **cold war** of the 1950s. He was elected New York's governor in 1954.

Hopper, Edward (1882–1967), artist. When other New York artists were painting street life, Hopper chose to show the city itself as a living thing. He saw beauty where others saw ugliness. Only after he retired from painting did he finally receive the praise of critics and collectors.

Horne, Lena (b. 1917), singer. A singing sensation at Harlem's Cotton Club in the 1930s, Horne was the first African-American woman to star with a white band in such nightclubs as the Savoy-Plaza and the Copacabana. She starred on Broadway in the 1950s and again in the 1980s, when her one-woman show ran for a record 333 performances.

Hughes, Charles Evans (1862–1948), politician. Hughes was governor of New York for four years before being appointed to the U.S. Supreme Court in 1910 by President William Taft. He served as secretary of state under Presidents Harding and Coolidge, then became chief justice of the Supreme Court in 1930.

Hughes, Langston (1902–1967), poet, author. One of the leading writers of the Harlem Renaissance of the 1920s, Hughes used hope and humor to shine a light on the way African Americans lived.

Langston Hughes

Irving, Washington (1783–1859), author. The first American writer widely read in the United States and Europe, Irving set many of his stories in the Hudson Valley. His best known works are *The Legend of Sleepy Hollow*, *Rip Van Winkle*, and *Diedrich Knickerbocker's History of New York*.

Jay, John (1745–1829), politician. A key figure in the American Revolution and a highly respected legal expert, Jay became the first chief justice of the U.S. Supreme Court in 1789. Six years later he became New York's second governor, then retired in 1801.

Joel, Billy (b. 1949), singer. Born in the Bronx, Joel displayed an early talent on the piano and began taking lessons at age four. During his career, Joel has sold more than 100 million albums worldwide, and has won 5 Grammys, the Grammy Legend Award in 1990, and numerous other songwriter awards. He is also a member of the Rock and Roll Hall of Fame.

Jolson, Al (1886–1950), singer. Jolson entertained New York audiences with his great singing. He starred in the first full-length "talking" movie, *The Jazz Singer*, in 1927.

Julia, Raul (1940–1994), actor. After moving to New York in the 1960s, Julia became one of the city's most well-known stage actors. From Broadway musicals to Shakespeare in the Park, he proved a Latino could achieve true stardom in the American theater.

Al Jolson

La Guardia, Fiorello (1882–1947), politician. As New York City's most famous mayor, La Guardia got the city through the Great Depression with humor, kindness, and a special talent for getting things done. His three terms were highlighted by huge improvements in the housing and welfare systems.

Lippmann, Walter (1889–1974), publisher, journalist. Lippmann was one of the most respected social **commentators** of the 1900s. He wrote for over 60 years. His column, "Today and Tomorrow," began in the *New York Herald Tribune*. Eventually, his writing was published in more than 250 newspapers in the United States and about 25 other nations. Lippmann won two **Pulitzer Prizes**.

Yo Yo Ma

Ma, Yo-Yo (b. 1955), cellist. When he moved with his family to New York at age seven, Ma had been giving cello recitals for two years. One of the youngest students ever to study at the Julliard School in New York City, he went on to record more than 50 albums and become one of history's greatest cellists.

Marx, Julius Henry "Groucho" (1890–1977), entertainer. Groucho Marx was a huge star on New York's **vaudeville** and Broadway stages with the Marx Brothers. They delighted in poking fun at anyone who took themselves too seriously. Their movies introduced their brand of comedy to the rest of the nation, and inspired many comedians.

Melville, Herman (1819–1891), author. *Moby Dick*, Melville's novel about a man obsessed with hunting down a white whale, was a hit when it was published in 1851. Melville quit writing soon after it was published and became a city customs inspector.

Miller, Arthur (1915–2005), author. One of New York's best playwrights in the 1950s and 1960s, Miller's works are still performed all over the world. His masterpiece, *Death of a Salesman*, is a classic of the American stage.

Anna "Grandma" Moses

Moses, Anna (1860–1961), artist. Born in 1860, Anna Moses did not start painting until 1936. Her simple, colorful paintings provided a glimpse into upstate life and created great interest in American folk art. She was best known as Grandma Moses.

Moses, Robert (1888–1981), state official. As New York City parks commissioner and head of the Triborough Bridge and Tunnel Authority, Moses changed the look of the city in the 1930s through the 1960s. Among his greatest achievements were the creation of the Jones Beach recreation complex, and both the 1939 and 1964 World's Fairs. Moses was also responsible for the construction of 13 bridges, 416 miles (670 kilometers) of modern roadways, and 658 playgrounds in the city.

Nash, Ogden (1902–1971), poet. A poet with a great sense of humor, Nash developed a loyal following while writing for the *New Yorker* in the 1930s. His funny and memorable poems lifted the spirits of his readers during the Great Depression, and he became one of America's most often quoted poets.

Rosie O'Donnell

O'Donnell, Rosie (b. 1962), entertainer. Born in Commack, Long Island, O'Donnell was her senior class president and prom queen. After deciding to become a standup comedian and taking her act on the road, O'Donnell won the *Star Search* television show competition five times. Her big acting break came when she starred in the hit movie *A League of Their Own*. O'Donnell hosted a daily talk show—*The Rosie O'Donnell Show*—from 1996 to 2002.

Olmsted, Frederick Law (1822–1903), landscape architect. Olmsted designed Manhattan's Central Park and Prospect Park in Brooklyn, as well as parks in Albany and Buffalo. After his New York triumphs, he went on to design more than 50 parks around the country, as well as the grounds of the U.S. Capitol in Washington, D.C.

Powell, Colin (b. 1937), military leader, politician. Powell entered the military during the Vietnam War (1957–1975) and rose rapidly to the rank of general. In 1989 he became the youngest person and first African American to be named chairman of the Joint Chiefs of Staff. Powell **masterminded** the Gulf War in 1991 and became secretary of state ten years later.

Colin Powell

Pulitzer, Joseph (1847–1911), journalist. A newspaper publisher who bought the *New York World* in 1883, Pulitzer gained fame for constructing the city's largest building and leading a campaign to bring the Statue of Liberty to New York. He funded the country's first journalism school at Columbia University. His name lives on with the Pulitzer Prize, which is awarded for literature, education, and public service.

Remington, Frederic (1861–1909), artist. After exploring the United States in the 1880s, Remington returned to his native New York and began painting from his sketches and memories. He completed more than 1,000 paintings and many sculptures of the American West. A museum dedicated to his work is located in Ogdensburg, New York.

Robinson, Jackie (1919–1972), athlete. In 1947 Robinson became the first African American to play baseball in the major leagues, playing for the Brooklyn Dodgers. For several years, he endured threats with silence and dignity, then began to speak out for **civil rights** and racial equality. By the time he retired in 1957, Robinson was one of the most admired New Yorkers in history.

Jackie Robinson

Rockefeller, John D. (1839–1937), **industrialist,** philanthropist. Born and raised in upstate New York, Rockefeller moved to Ohio with his family in the 1850s, where he started a grain and grocery business and grew rich during the Civil War (1861–1865). He got into the oil business in the early 1860s, and started the Standard Oil Company. By the time Rockefeller returned to New York in 1883, his company was producing four of every five barrels of oil in the United States.

Rockefeller, Nelson (1908–1979), politician. The grandson of John D. Rockefeller, Nelson Rockefeller was elected governor of New York in 1958 and served four terms during difficult social and economic times. A great believer in the power of education, he added 43 campuses to the state university system. He also created 50 new state parks. In 1974 Rockefeller agreed to serve as President Gerald Ford's vice president after President Richard Nixon resigned.

Roebling, John Augustus (1806–1869), civil engineer. An immigrant from Prussia, Roebling invented the super-strong wire cable that made construction of large suspension bridges possible. After building the span over Niagara Falls in 1855, he was hired to design the Brooklyn Bridge. A construction accident led to his death in 1869, leaving his son, Washington, to complete the project 14 years later.

Roosevelt, Eleanor (1884–1962), social activist. Known as our country's most politically active first lady, Roosevelt began working with the

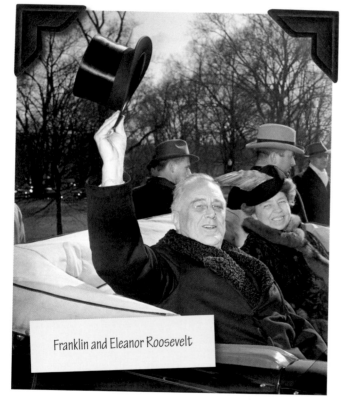

Franklin and Eleanor Roosevelt

Women's Trade Union League and League of Women Voters several years before her husband, Franklin, was elected president in 1933. She became the eyes, ears, and conscience of the Roosevelt administration—fighting for the rights of minorities, children, and the poor.

Roosevelt, Franklin Delano (1882– 1945), politician. Roosevelt contracted **polio** in 1921, but he still served over 40 years in politics. He was elected New York's governor in 1928. In 1932 he was elected U.S. president and introduced several programs to help the country survive the Great Depression. Roosevelt was re-elected three times.

Roosevelt, Theodore (1858–1919), politician. Roosevelt started as New York City's police commissioner and was later elected governor. He was known for battling **corruption**. He was elected vice president of the U.S. in 1900. He became U.S. president after the death of William McKinley in 1901 and was elected to a second term in 1904. Roosevelt and Franklin D. Roosevelt were fifth cousins. Theodore Roosevelt died from complications of **malaria** in 1919.

Ruth, George Herman "Babe" (1895–1948), athlete. After growing up in Baltimore and starting his baseball career in Boston, Ruth was sold in 1920 to the Yankees for the then-incredible sum of $125,000. Ruth's hitting and personality made him the most famous athlete in the world at that time. During his 15 years in New York, "the Sultan of Swat" hit 659 home runs and led his team to seven American League pennants.

Babe Ruth

Sagan, Carl (1934–1996), astronomer. Beginning in the 1950s, Sagan was a consultant and advisor to NASA (National Aeronautics and Space Administration.) He was among the first to propose that life could have existed on Mars. Sagan helped solve the mysteries of the high temperature of Venus, the seasonal changes on Mars, and the reddish haze of Titan, Saturn's moon. Sagan also won the Pulitzer Prize for his writings about space.

J.D. Salinger

Salinger, J.D. (b. 1919), author. Salinger's 1951 book *The Catcher in the Rye*, written and set in New York City, influenced three generations of teenagers and brought him fame. A very private man, he stopped publishing in 1965 and retired to New Hampshire.

Salk, Jonas (1914–1995), physician, researcher. In the decade following World War II, thousands of children contracted polio each year, causing widespread panic in the nation's cities. In 1955 Salk introduced a life-saving **serum** (liquid) to prevent the crippling disease.

Sarnoff, David (1891–1971), radio and television pioneer. Understanding the potential of wireless broadcasting, Sarnoff predicted that one day there would be a "radio music box" in every American home. By 1926, he was head of the National Broadcasting Company (NBC), and later introduced television to the public at the 1939 World's Fair.

Seward, William (1801–1872), politician. Seward fought against slavery as a U.S. congressman and as Abraham Lincoln's secretary of state. In 1867 he purchased Alaska from the Russians even though his fellow politicians thought he was making a big mistake.

Smith, Joseph (1805–1844), religious leader. Smith claimed to have been visited by God in the city of Palmyra when he was 15. Ten years later, in 1830, he published *The Book of Mormon* and founded the Church of Jesus Christ of Latter-day Saints. Today, the Mormons are based in Salt Lake City, Utah.

Stanton, Elizabeth Cady (1815–1902), social activist. Stanton believed that American women were treated unfairly by the rest of society. In 1848 she called for a convention to discuss the conditions of women, and 300 people made their way to her hometown of Seneca Falls. From that meeting sprang the women's rights movement.

Elizabeth Cady Stanton

Steinem, Gloria (b. 1934), **feminist**, political activist. A journalist and women's rights activist in the 1960s, Steinem first gained attention as a columnist for *New York Magazine*. As the founding editor of *MS.* magazine in 1972, she became one of America's most well-known feminist leaders.

Streisand, Barbra (b. 1942), entertainer. Over her 40-year career, Streisand has achieved great success as a singer, actor, and director. She has been awarded numerous Tony, Grammy, Emmy, and Academy Awards for her work.

Truth, Sojourner (1797–1883), antislavery and women's rights **advocate**. Truth was born as Isabella Baumfree, a slave in upstate New York. She was known to audiences from New England to Washington, D.C., and continued to fight for the rights of African Americans after the Civil War (1861–1865). In 1850 a book about her experiences, *The Narrative of Sojourner Truth: A Northern Slave*, was published.

Tubman, Harriet (1820–1913), **abolitionist**. Tubman was a creator of the **Underground Railroad** for escaped slaves. She herself escaped from her Maryland owner, eventually settled in the town of Auburn, and lived there until her death at age 93.

Van Buren, Martin (1782–1862), politician. After 12 years of service as attorney general, senator, and governor, Van Buren became U.S. secretary of state for President Andrew Jackson, and later Jackson's vice president. Van Buren became president himself in 1836. He was opposed to the spread of slavery, against the **annexation** of Texas as a state, and supported a war with the Seminole Indians. He was not reelected in 1840.

Harriet Tubman

Vanderbilt, Cornelius (1794–1877), shipping and railroad businessperson. The "father" of New York's most famous wealthy family, Vanderbilt began building his fortune by running ferry boats from Staten Island to Manhattan, and later by heading the New York Central Railroad. The family built several magnificent mansions, founded Vanderbilt University in Tennessee, and gave generously to the arts and sciences.

Wharton, Edith (1862–1937), author. Wharton wrote about New York City's rich and powerful people. Her books were extremely popular, and in 1921 she became the first woman to win the Pulitzer Prize.

White, Stanford (1853–1906), architect. A self-taught architect, White designed several New York landmarks, including the Washington Arch, Metropolitan Club, and the first Madison Square Garden. He also designed jewelry, furniture, and magazine covers.

Edith Wharton

Whitman, Walt (1819–1892), poet and journalist. Whitman and his poetry were considered crude by some. With the support of Ralph Waldo Emerson, however, his *Leaves of Grass* made him popular nationwide after it was published in 1855.

Woolworth, Frank (1852–1919), businessperson. Woolworth opened the first five-and-dime store in Utica in 1879, and by 1905, the idea had caught on enough to start a national chain of stores. By the time he died, Woolworth owned more than 1,000 stores and had built the tallest building in New York City.

Map of New York

N W E S

Plattsburgh
Lake Champlain
Lake Placid
Adirondack
Mountains
Ticonderoga
Watertown
Lake George
Lake Ontario
Oswego
Oneida Lake
Rome
Great
Sacandaga
Lake
Niagara Falls
Rochester
Syracuse
Utica
Buffalo
Seneca Falls
Mohawk River
Schenectady
Canandaigua
Lake
Skaneateles Lake
Cooperstown
Lake Erie
Dansville
Seneca
Lake
Cayuga Lake
Albany
Genessee River
Ithaca
Susquehanna River
Hudson River
Hudson
Chautauqua Lake
Finger Lakes
Nat'l Forest
Binghamton
Catskill
Mountains
Kingston
Poughkeepsie
White Plains
Montauk
New York City
Fire Island
National Seashore

0   50 miles
0   50 km

⊙ capital
• cities
〰 river
◼ National Forest
◻ National Park
— state line

CANADA
Maine
Vermont
New
Hampshire
New York
Massachusetts
Rhode Island
Connecticut
Ohio
Pennsylvania
New
Jersey
Atlantic
Ocean

Glossary

abolish do away with or put an end to

abolitionist person who wanted to ban slavery

activist someone who publicly supports a cause

advocate someone who argues for a cause

amateur person who takes part in sports or occupations not for pay

annexation adding something to something else so the piece becomes part of the whole

assassinate murder an important person by surprise attack

borough one of the five political divisions of New York City

broadside sheet of paper printed on one side

brownstone building made out of reddish-brown sandstone

canal artificial waterway for boats

census annual count of population and the gathering of information about that population

chronicle historical account of events arranged in order of time

civil rights rights of personal liberty guaranteed by the U.S. Constitution

Civil Rights movement demand for equal rights for African Americans

cold war state of conflict between the U.S. and the Soviet Union that stopped short of actual battles

commentator person who reports and discusses news events

composer writer of music

conductor person who leads a musical group

conscience knowledge of right and wrong and a feeling that one should do what is right

corner take control of

corruption lack of honesty

crusader one who takes part in a campaign to get things changed for the better

culture/cultural ideas, skills, arts, and a way of life of a certain people at a certain time

deportation act of forcing someone to leave the country

diplomat someone who works to maintain relations between governments of different countries

discriminate treat people unfairly based on their differences from others

diverse/diversity having variety

dominate to have a controlling position or power

duel combat between two persons fought with deadly weapons and with witnesses present

economic relating to the production, distribution, and consumption of goods and services

emancipation setting free from control or slavery

ethnic/ethnicity belonging to a group with a particular culture

famine time when food is scarce and people are starving

federal highest U.S. goverment

feminist someone who participates in organized activities promoting equal rights for women

frontiersman person living on the edge of a settled part of a country

Great Depression ten-year period of economic hardship starting in 1929, in which unemployment was high and many businesses failed

heritage something that comes from one's ancestors

humidity degree of wetness in the atmosphere

immigrant one who moves to another country to settle

industrialist person who owns or manages an industry

industry group of businesses that offer a similar product or service

injustice violation of a person's rights

legislature governmental body that makes and changes laws

lieutenant governor second in command of a state, after the governor

malaria disease spread by the bite of a mosquito

manipulating managing skillfully and with the intent to be dishonest

mastermind director and creative thinker for a project

metropolitan area surrounding a large city

multicultural of, relating to, or made up of several different cultures

orator public speaker noted for skill and power in speaking

paralyzed unable to move or feel part of one's body

peasant farmer owning a small amount of land

philanthropist person who gives generously to help other people

polio once-common virus mostly affecting children and sometimes causing paralysis

port harbor for ships to load and unload cargo

prejudice unfair judgment formed before any facts are examined

prospect possibility

Pulitzer Prize award given in the United States in several fields, including literature, education, and public service

reformer someone who tries to make something better

renovation to put in good condition again

robber baron someone who takes things away from others using secrecy and trickery

rural having to do with the country or farmland

serum liquid used to cure diseases

statistic quantity computed from a sample

subway underground transportation system

tapestry different people brought together to make one large group that works together

thrive to do very well

transatlantic extending across the Atlantic Ocean

transformed changed completely

treason crime of trying to overthrow the government

turmoil confused state or condition

tycoon very powerful and wealthy businessperson

Underground Railroad system of cooperation by antislavery people in the U.S. before 1863 by which runaway slaves were secretly helped to reach freedom

vaudeville theatrical entertainment made up of songs, dances, and comic arts

vigilante citizen who arrests and punishes criminals without any legal authority to do so

women's rights movement demand for equal rights for women

Find Out More

Further Reading

Kupperberg, Paul. *A Primary Source History of the Colony of New York*. New York: Rosen Publishing, 2006.

Website

http://pbskids.org/bigapplehistory/index-flash.html
Learn more about the Big Apple on this fascinating site!

Index